CLASSIC CARS
AN IMAGINATION LIBRARY SERIES

THE STORY OF THE

Jeep

by Jim Mezzanotte

GARETH**STEVENS**
GS
PUBLISHING
A WRC Media Company

Please visit our web site at: www.garethstevens.com
For a free color catalog describing Gareth Stevens Publishing's
list of high-quality books and multimedia programs,
call 1-800-542-2595 (USA) or 1-800-387-3178 (Canada).
Gareth Stevens Publishing's fax: (414) 332-3567.

Library of Congress Cataloging-in-Publication Data

Mezzanotte, Jim.
    The story of the Jeep / by Jim Mezzanotte.
        p. cm. — (Classic cars: an imagination library series)
    Includes bibliographical references and index.
    ISBN 0-8368-4536-6 (lib. bdg.)
    1. Jeep automobile—History. I. Title. II. Series.
    TL215.J44M48   2005
    629.222'2—dc22   2004062582

First published in 2005 by
Gareth Stevens Publishing
A WRC Media Company
330 West Olive Street, Suite 100
Milwaukee, WI 53212 USA

Text: Jim Mezzanotte
Cover design and page layout: Scott M. Krall
Series editors: JoAnn Early Macken and Mark J. Sachner
Picture Researcher: Diane Laska-Swanke

Photo credits: Cover, p. 9 Courtesy of www.northstarwillys.com; pp. 5, 7 © National Motor Museum;
pp. 11, 17, 19 Courtesy of Leo Schneider; pp. 13, 21 © Ron Kimball; p. 15 Moshe ben-Shimon

Printed in the United States of America

1 2 3 4 5 6 7 8 9 09 08 07 06 05

*Front cover: At first, only soldiers used Jeeps.
But through the years, all kinds of people have
discovered the amazing things Jeeps can do.*

TABLE OF CONTENTS

Words that appear in the glossary are printed in **boldface** type the first time they occur in the text.

THE FIRST JEEPS

It was the year 1940. World War II had started. Soon, the United States would be in the war. The U.S. Army needed a new **vehicle**. It asked some companies to create a new **design**. A company named Willys-Overland had the best design.

The new vehicle was small and light, but it was strong. It could hold a lot of weight. The vehicle had four-wheel drive. Its engine turned all four wheels. The vehicle had great **traction**. It could go over rocky ground and through streams.

People called these vehicles "Jeeps." Thousands were built for the war. Jeeps became famous!

When the first Jeeps were built, there were no other vehicles like them. This Willys Jeep was made in 1943, during World War II.

A HERO NAMED JEEP

Jeeps were a big help during World War II. Some Jeeps carried weapons. Others carried wounded soldiers. Jeeps could go anywhere. They drove through deserts and jungles and mountains. Jeeps hardly ever broke down. They helped win the war. Soldiers loved Jeeps!

No one is sure how the Jeep got its name. Some people think it came from a comic strip. Back then, *Popeye* was a popular comic strip. In the comic strip, there was a magical creature, Eugene the Jeep. Eugene did amazing things, just like the real-life Jeep.

Soldiers on motorcycles follow a Jeep during World War II. Like motorcycles, Jeeps could travel on rough ground. But they could also carry a lot of men and equipment.

OUT OF THE ARMY

After the war, Willys kept making Jeeps. Some of these Jeeps were for the army. But the company also built a **civilian** Jeep. Anybody could buy one.

This new Jeep was called the CJ-2A. The letters "CJ" stood for civilian Jeep. This Jeep was similar to the army jeep. It was rugged and dependable. It had four-wheel drive. The Jeep could go places where other vehicles got stuck. It was good for all kinds of jobs. People began buying this new Jeep. The Jeep was not just for the army anymore!

The CJ-3A came after the CJ-2A. This CJ-3A was built in 1950. By then, many people had begun using Jeeps for tough civilian jobs.

THE CLASSIC JEEP

In 1954, Willys made a new Jeep. It was called the CJ-5. This Jeep was different from earlier models. It had a rounder shape. It was larger, so it had more room for passengers. The CJ-5 was stronger and more powerful, too.

Farmers and other workers bought the Jeep CJ-5. Other people bought it, too. They liked driving the Jeep off the road. The Jeep was not just for work. It was for fun, too. People used Jeeps to go camping, hunting, and fishing.

The CJ-5 was made until 1983. It is the most successful Jeep of all time!

With the tough CJ-5, people began having off-road adventures. These Jeep owners are having fun riding through some rugged hills.

THE FIRST SUV

Today, many people drive SUVs. "SUV" stands for sport **utility** vehicle. An SUV is roomy and comfortable like a car. Like a truck, it is also strong and good for carrying things. An SUV usually has four-wheel drive. It can drive off the road.

Some people think Jeep made the first SUV. It came out in 1949. It looked like a big station wagon, but it had four-wheel drive. A better model came out in 1962. It was called the Wagoneer. The Wagoneer had a smoother body shape. It was comfortable and easy to drive. Now, whole families could travel in a Jeep.

This modern SUV is a 1996 Jeep Cherokee. In many ways, it is similar to the early Wagoneers. It keeps people comfortable, even when traveling through water.

JEEPS AT WORK

Jeeps have been used for many different jobs. People have used Jeeps on farms and at construction sites. Jeeps have pulled all kinds of equipment. They have carried heavy loads. They have been used by fire departments and police departments. They have worked at airports. Jeeps have even been used as taxis.

For many years, **postal** workers used a special Jeep. They delivered mail with it. This Jeep had a big sliding door. It also had the steering wheel on the right side instead of the left side! A postal worker could stay in the Jeep and still deliver mail.

Like postal Jeeps, this Jeep has the steering wheel on the right side. The parking checker can stay in it while handing out parking tickets!

BETTER JEEPS

By the 1970s, a different company made Jeeps. It was called American Motors. The company improved the Jeep. Jeeps got better brakes and steering. They had **roll bars** for safety. Some Jeeps had big V-8 engines. The engines had eight **cylinders** for a lot of power. Jeeps got bigger, and they had more room inside.

American Motors also created the Cherokee. This SUV became very popular. The Cherokee is still made today.

The Wrangler came out in the late 1980s. This Jeep was a new design. It looked a little different from earlier Jeeps. It was more comfortable, but it was still tough!

This Jeep is a CJ-7 Renegade. It has a powerful engine, big tires, and a roll bar. This Jeep can travel through some very rough places.

FOUR-WHEELING!

Many Jeep owners love to drive off the road. They call it four-wheeling because the Jeeps have four-wheel drive. They travel in the woods or in the desert. They go through water. They climb steep hills. Some people **modify** their Jeeps. These Jeeps have extra big tires and are high off the ground.

Some Jeep owners race off the road. Other Jeep owners just like to go camping. They have fun driving on different trails.

When people go four-wheeling, they have to be careful. They should not harm plants or animals. They have to be ready for problems, too. Even Jeeps can get stuck!

This Jeep's oversize tires and four-wheel drive help it get in and out of places no ordinary car would dare to go!

JEEPS FOR TODAY

Today, Jeeps are still being made. DaimlerChrysler now makes them. Today's Jeeps have powerful, **efficient** engines. They have better **suspension** for a smooth ride. Some Jeeps are as comfortable as cars. All Jeeps can handle rough roads.

One Jeep model is called the Wrangler Rubicon. Some people think it is the best Jeep ever! It is named after the Rubicon Trail in California. This off-road trail is very tough. The Rubicon was designed to go four-wheeling. It has many **heavy-duty** parts.

Jeeps have been around for more than sixty years. They are still ready to go anywhere!

This modern Jeep is a 2004 Wrangler Rubicon. It has special features for handling the toughest off-road adventures.

MORE TO READ AND VIEW

Books (Nonfiction)
Desert Racers. Roaring Rides (series). Tracy Maurer (Rourke Publishing)
Jeep Color History. Steve Stratham (Motorbooks International)
Jeeps. Cruisin' (series). Thomas Streissguth (Capstone Press)
Off-Road Vehicles. Designed for Success (series). Ian Graham (Heinemann Library)

Books (Fiction)
Cheap Jeep. Janice Gill (Aro Books, Inc.)

Videos (Nonfiction)
Jeep. (A&E Entertainment)
The Visual History of Cars: Jeep. (MPI Home Video)
Wild About Wheels: The Unstoppable Soldier — Jeep. (UAV Corporation)

PLACES TO WRITE AND VISIT

Here are three places to contact for more information:

Heritage Region Jeep Alliance
PO Box 1766
Cranberry Twp, PA 16066
www.hrja.org

Walter P. Chrysler Museum
One Chrysler Drive
Auburn Hills, MI
48326-2778
1-888-456-1924
www.chryslerheritage.com

Willys America
P.O. Box 538
Cazadero, CA 95421
www.willysamerica.com

WEB SITES

Web sites change frequently, but we believe the following web sites are going to last. You can also use good search engines, such as **Yahooligans!** [www.yahooligans.com] or **Google** [www.google.com], to find more information about Jeeps. Here are some keywords to help you: *four wheeling, four-wheel drive, Grand Cherokee, Jeep, off road, Rubicon trail, Wagoneer, and Willys.*

www.californiajeeper.com/barney/review.htm

On this web site, you can read a short history of military and civilian Jeeps, and see some pictures of Jeeps, too. The site also has information about off road trails.

www.film.queensu.ca/CJ3B/Poster.html

This web site is a history of the Jeep. It has pictures of many Jeeps through the years, plus information about them.

www.hrja.org/jeep.htm

The Heritage Region Jeep Alliance is a club for people who love Jeeps! This part of the club's web site is a history of the Jeep. It explains how the Jeep was first developed.

www.jeep.com/4x4/index.html?context=homepage&type=tab

Go 4X4 is part of the official Jeep web site. It has information about four-wheeling, off road trails, and Jeep events.

www.offroad.com/jeep/classicjeep/index.htm

This web page is part of the Off-Road.com web site. It has a history of the military Jeep and information about many Jeep models, with pictures.

www.webejeepin.com/Jeep_History/Jeep History.htm

Visit this site for information about many kinds of Jeeps, including the first military and civilian Jeeps, Jeep SUVs, and later models. This site also has many pictures of Jeeps.

23

GLOSSARY

You can find these words on the pages listed. Reading a word in a sentence helps you understand it even better.

civilian (suh-VIL-yun) — not part of the military. 8

cylinders (SIL-in-durz) — tubes inside an engine where gas explodes, giving the engine power. 16

design (dee-ZINE) — a plan for building something. 4, 16, 20

efficient (eeh-FISH-unt) — able to do something without wasting time or energy. 20

heavy-duty (heh-vee DOO-tee) — strong and reliable for rough conditions. 20

modify (MOD-if-eye) — make changes to something. 18

postal (POE-stull) — having to do with the post office or delivering mail. 14

roll bars (ROLE barz) — metal bars in a vehicle that protect people if the vehicle rolls over. 16

suspension (suh-SPEN-shun) — the parts that connect the wheels to a car and help the car go smoothly over bumps. 20

traction (TRAC-shun) — a vehicle's ability to grip the ground. 4

utility (yu-TIL-uh-tee) — designed to be useful for certain jobs. 12

vehicle (VEE-hick-ull) — something that transports people or things. 4, 8, 12

INDEX